BLM Technical Note 436

Recommendations for Improved Raptor Nest Monitoring in Association with Oil and Gas Development Activities

Jeff P. Smith[1], Steven J. Slater, and Mike C. Neal

HawkWatch International, Inc.
2240 South 900 East
Salt Lake City, Utah 84106

[1] Phone: (801) 484-6808 x109
Email: jsmith@hawkwatch.org

Prepared for:
U.S. Department of Interior,
Bureau of Land Management
Utah State Office, Salt Lake City,
Wyoming State Office, Cheyenne, and
Colorado State Office, Lakewood

Table of Contents

Abstract v

Acknowledgements vii

Introduction 1

Data Standards and Record Keeping 3
   Terminology 3
   Nest Naming Conventions 3
   Location-Data Standards 4
   Nest-Cluster versus Nest-Centric Monitoring 5
   Availability and Quality of Ancillary Data 5

Survey Design and Rigor 7
   Nest-Cluster versus Nest-Centric Monitoring 7
   Baseline Monitoring 7
   Survey Extent and Timing 7
   Problems HWI Identified Concerning
      Raptor-Related Management of
      OG Development Activities 8

Recommendations for Improved
   Monitoring 11
   Survey Methods 17
   Continued Monitoring 17
   Recommendations on the Recording
      and Storage of Data 18

Literature Cited 19

Appendix A. Example field datasheets
   for raptor nest monitoring 21

Raptor nest monitoring may be utilized to guide federal land-use planning, protect raptors, and assess the potential impacts of oil and gas development projects. The utility of monitoring programs is compromised when a program is not designed to address specific objectives and when the survey protocols are incomplete or applied inconsistently. HawkWatch International (HWI) and the Bureau of Land Management (BLM) encountered such monitoring limitations during the Raptor Radii Research Project, which attempted to analyze historic raptor nesting data from Utah and Wyoming in relation to past energy development activities on BLM-administered lands and to identify potential sites for experimental testing of nest-protection buffers. We summarize the difficulties encountered during this research project and provide our (HWI) recommendations for improvement of future nest-monitoring programs to be conducted in association with oil and gas development activities. We identify the basic problems HWI encountered with regard to the nature of available data, which can be divided into three primary issues: 1) basic data standards and record keeping; 2) survey design and rigor; and 3) availability of ancillary data. We then provide a series of HWI recommendations designed to guide future monitoring programs in ways that, if implemented as standard practice, should substantially improve the potential for achieving robust future evaluations of oil and gas development or other land-use-change impacts to nesting raptors. Regardless of their specific application, the recommendations for improved monitoring should be of value to any raptor nest-monitoring program implemented on federal lands. We also identify links to examples of field datasheets and a relational database system designed to accommodate a comprehensive annual program of raptor nest monitoring, and provide recommendations for storage of collected monitoring data.

Acknowledgements

This document was created to address raptor nest-survey and data limitations the authors encountered while executing Phase I of the "Raptor Radii Research Project," funded by the U.S. Department of Energy through the BLM Utah State Office (BLM Assistance Agreement JSA065003). This document benefited from reviews and suggestions provided by the Raptor Radii Project BLM Steering Committee, which included Dave Mills (BLM Utah, Richfield Field Office), Steve Madsen (BLM Utah State Office), Dave Roberts (BLM Wyoming State Office), and Wes Anderson (BLM Colorado State Office). Additional semi-independent reviews were provided by vested individuals, including Chris Colt (Fishlake National Forest, formerly UDWR Price Field Office) and Mark Fuller (U.S. Geological Survey, Idaho). Further independent reviews were provided by Michael Kochert (U.S. Geological Survey, Idaho), Gwyn McKee (Thunderbird-Jones & Stokes, Inc., Wyoming), and Jim Watson (Washington Department of Fish and Wildlife).

Raptor nest monitoring should play an integral part in wildlife inventory programs carried out on federal lands. Properly designed and implemented nest-monitoring programs can aid federal land managers during resource planning and increase the likelihood of compliance with the protections extended to nesting raptors by the Migratory Bird Treaty Act and Bald and Golden Eagle Protection Act. Additionally, properly designed and executed monitoring programs can be used to assess the potential impacts of various land-use activities. That said, monitoring programs lacking proper and consistent implementation can greatly compromise the value of the data collected. A recent effort by HawkWatch International (HWI) and the Bureau of Land Management (BLM) to assess the potential impacts of oil and gas (OG) development on nesting raptors was particularly insightful in this regard. The project, called the "Raptor Radii Research Project," was designed to be carried out in two phases. Phase I sought to utilize historic nesting data to identify potential correlations between nest-activity patterns and OG development activities in the BLM Price Field Office (FO) in southeastern Utah and the BLM Rawlins FO in south-central Wyoming (Smith et al. 2010). During the course of compiling existing nesting data from each study area, we discovered a number of inadequacies and inconsistencies, related primarily to problems with the survey terminology and methodology applied over the years, which significantly hampered the analyses and likely compromised the insight achievable from the data. We also identified additional difficulties while attempting to locate potential study sites for an experimental assessment of OG-related nest disturbance thresholds as part of Phase II of this research project. Unfortunately, our inability to identify areas experiencing OG development that also contained reasonably complete raptor nest inventories and histories was a contributing factor in the abandonment of the Phase II effort.

In light of our experiences during the Raptor Radii Research Project, we have prepared this technical note in order to summarize the problems we encountered, outline exactly how they hampered our analyses, and translate the resulting insights into recommendations for improved future monitoring, specifically in relation to potential OG development projects. It is important to reflect at the outset that exactly what standards are applied in developing a new monitoring program depends entirely on the stated objectives for implementing the program. Numerous references are available in the scientific and statistical literature to help guide formulation of monitoring objectives and applicable methodological standards. It is not our goal for this discussion to comprise a "Monitoring 101" treatment. Rather, our intent is to focus specifically on the problems we encountered with the existing datasets in relation to achieving the objective of evaluating the effects of OG development on nesting raptors in the two study areas, and to recommend improved standards to help guide future monitoring oriented toward such an objective.

Terminology

Steenhof and Newton (2007) effectively articulate the importance of standardized terminology and careful attention to defining terms used to code nest-status and productivity observations. We found great inconsistencies in the terminology used over the years to code nesting events in the Rawlins dataset, in particular, and more generally found that, based on notes recorded in the available databases, that various nest-status designations were not always consistently applied due to variations in field personnel and attendant differences in interpretation or levels of rigor in applying those designations. For example, in the Rawlins dataset, it became clear that designations of "used" and "active" were often used inter-changeably without clarity as to whether or not egg-laying was actually confirmed (accurate definition of "active," indicating an actual breeding attempt), such that it was frequently impossible to differentiate between occupied but inactive nests/territories and those in which a breeding attempt actually occurred. This lack of clarity especially hampered our ability to designate confidently many historical nest records as truly representing breeding attempts. Moreover, even accurate designation of nest records as representing an "occupied" scenario was problematic due to inconsistencies in what surveyors considered evidence of territory occupation. For example, the basis for designating a nest/territory as occupied was often limited to one brief sighting of a single bird in the general vicinity of a nest/territory, whereas a more rigorous and appropriate standard would be multiple sightings of at least one territorial, breeding-age adult in the immediate vicinity of the relevant nest cluster (*sensu* Smith et al. 2009). The same basic problems applied to application of the designation "tended" in the Price surveys, especially because these classifications were based on brief, single visits to nests. The highly variable conditions that contributed to a particular nest being classified as "used" for our analyses, compared to the more concrete evidence required for a designation of "active," may have contributed to the typical modeling trend we observed in our analyses of data from both study areas. That is, we typically identified more competing top models of nest-cluster use compared to top models of cluster activity (see Smith et al. 2009). For example, for Price-area Red-tailed Hawks (*Buteo jamaicensis*) we identified 18 top "use" models, but only one top "activity" model.

Steenhof and Newton (2007) carefully outline appropriate terminology and standards for accurate designation of nest/territory status and productivity, and therefore we do not need to reiterate those here. The important point is that, before any monitoring program is instituted, applicable standardized terminology should be clearly articulated with unambiguous definitions, those standards should be rigorously applied throughout the course of the monitoring program, and metadata reflecting those standards should always accompany any resulting datasets. If new insight generated from future research dictates a need to change those standards, a careful record of the change must be included in the metadata associated with the database and a clear "cross-walk" articulated to describe the relationships between the old and new standards. Ideally, to render data of maximum utility, it is important to carefully distinguish among unoccupied nest clusters, occupied clusters in which no breeding attempt (eggs laid) occurred, occupied clusters in which a failed breeding attempt occurred, and occupied clusters in which a successful breeding attempt occurred. Of course, careful attention to and consistent application of standardized definitions of "occupied" and "successful" also is required, with the latter typically equating to successful rearing of at least one nestling to at least 80% of the average fledging age for the species (Steenhof and Newton 2007). Determining the actual number of chicks reared to 80% of fledging age would comprise the final ingredient for comprehensive monitoring by yielding an estimate of "productivity."

Nest Naming Conventions

Developing appropriate standards for uniquely identifying specific nest sites also is critically important. Several acceptable approaches are possible. In this regard, the difficulty we encountered with the Rawlins naming system concerned incorporation of a species designator in the nest name. The problem arises because many nests are used by more than one species over the years. As a result, some year-specific nest records in the Rawlins dataset were confused because no consistent method was applied to identify when a given year's record involved a species different from that for which the nest was named initially. In other words, in several cases we assumed that a given record related to the species identified in the nest code, when in fact careful perusing of miscellaneous notes associated with the record ultimately revealed that in fact another species used the nest that year. For this reason, nest numbers should not include any reference to the species, with that information relegated to other year-specific fields in the relational database system. In the case of the Price dataset, no species designator was incorporated in the nest numbers, but problems still arose in tracking use by multiple species due to a simple data-structure issue. The initial 2006 dataset we obtained included status records for all survey years, but included only one species designator, which we discovered belatedly applied only to the most recent year in which the nest was active and the species confirmed. In other words, if the species using the nest changed sometime during the survey period, information about the earlier species was effectively lost in the 2006 file (although recovered once we finally obtained all of the original, complete, year-specific datasets).

Beyond the species issue, our experience suggests that incorporating some method of systematic naming of individual nests is desirable. For example, nests in the Price dataset simply were assigned sequential nest IDs based on the order the nest was entered into the database. Although the reason is unclear, it became apparent that IDs given to a substantial number of Price nests in 1998 (the first year of helicopter surveys) were associated with different nests in the subsequent years. We were able to rectify this issue by inspecting the spatial relationship between individual nests in a Geographic Information System (GIS). We suggest that some manner of geographic designation be incorporated in the name to facilitate efficient tracking of records and nests on the landscape, and for helping to rectify problems when errors in nest coordinates are discovered. For example, in the Rawlins database, individual nests were given a unique nest ID based on the township-range-section (TRS) location of the nest, and then a unique number that reflected sequential numbering within that section only (e.g., Nest 14911201 would be the first nest identified in Township 14, Range 91, Section 12).

Another example approach that works well is the convention HWI adopted for its Great Basin Raptor Nest Survey (e.g., see Smith and Hutchins 2006, 2007), where the nest-naming standard incorporates an initial four-letter code indicating the name of the 7.5′ topographic quad map in which the nest occurs, followed by a unique number that reflects sequential numbering within that quad only. In our experience, although the spatial resolution of the HWI naming convention is coarser than the section-specific naming in the Rawlins dataset, a potential problem with the latter is that standard topographic maps used for navigation do not always include complete TRS delineations, such that it is not always possible to easily identify and track the TRS in which a given nest occurs, but it is always possible to easily locate the topographic quad.

Location-Data Standards

Advancements in Global Positioning System (GPS) technology in the last 10–15 years have greatly improved our ability to locate nests accurately using relatively inexpensive and efficient handheld devices. The lack of such technology hampered accurate mapping during the early survey years in the Rawlins study area; however, despite the availability of appropriate technology for at least the past 10 years or so, no GPS coordinates have ever been collected for any of the nests in the Rawlins study area. Instead, all nest locations were based strictly on hand mapping of the approximate locations on 7.5′ quad maps. Although the inherent accuracy of standard 7.5′ quad maps (±40 ft or 12.2 m; see http://erg.usgs. gov/isb/pubs/factsheets/fs17199.html) is only marginally worse than that of typical, currently available handheld GPS units (typically ±3–5 m), when compounded with the inaccuracy of subjective hand mapping of apparent locations and deriving coordinates from the map, the error associated with hand mapping is likely on the order of at least 10 times greater than with use of basic GPS technology, and may amount to inaccuracies of 50 m or more. Such error may not represent a problem with regard to effective return visits to nests in low nest-density situations; however, absent clear photographic records, it can render impossible the task of accurately distinguishing among multiple nests that are tightly clustered, which is often the case within Ferruginous Hawk (*Buteo regalis*) nesting territories, for example. Additionally, mapping inaccuracies were partially responsible for our inability to use digital elevation models and GIS to assess how the visibility of OG developments from individual nests may affect raptor responses in this study. Even relatively small location discrepancies can greatly alter the landscape visible from a given three-dimensional point, especially when nests are located in areas of substantial topographic relief (e.g., on cliff faces).

Although not a problem in the context of our Phase I investigations, during our Phase II planning efforts carried out in the Vernal, Utah and Meeker, Colorado study areas, we encountered GPS technology-related difficulties driven by the inconsistent use of mapping datums and, more importantly, a failure to note the particular datum used. Inconsistent use of the NAD27 and NAD83 datum standards, for example, can result in mismatch errors of >200 m when using the UTM coordinate system. Consistency of use and maintaining a clear record of the datum standard used is of greatest importance (software to convert among datums is readily available), but with regard to the choice of datum, one other issue of importance to consider is matching the GPS data against other tools used to facilitate navigation. If handheld GIS computers or advanced GPS models with built-in topographic maps are available, the GPS/computer combination may be all that is needed for effective navigation, in which case the datum used does not matter (as long as the chosen datum is recorded and consistently used). Such technology can be very expensive, however, and often the visual scale and resolution of view screens on such devices can hamper easy navigation across broad landscapes. The readily available and more typical approach is to combine use of GPS technology with navigation using topographic maps. In this case, the choice of datum makes a big difference, because most 7.5′ quad maps still utilize the older NAD27 datum.

Nest-Cluster versus Nest-Centric Monitoring

As discussed further below, it is essential that monitoring of nesting activity be based on a territory or "nest-cluster" (see Smith et al. 2010) approach rather than a nest-centric approach. Neither the Price nor Rawlins databases made available to us were designed to accommodate designation of nest-cluster affiliations. Such should be a fundamental component of any database of raptor nest histories because, once identified through appropriate means, it provides essential information for future surveyors to consider as they comb the landscape for activity. It was apparent from our inspection of the Price and Rawlins databases that field personnel were often unaware of the potential association between individual nests and larger clusters. For example, in Price, all the nests in a particular cluster (i.e., spatially grouped nests) were rarely surveyed in the same year, even when each of the individual nests was known from previous years. This clearly could have affected our analyses, as we were forced to assign status designations to clusters based on this incomplete data. Of course, complete surveying of all nests within a cluster is less of an issue when definite signs of activity are documented at a particular nest, but may be a serious issue when this is not the case. For example, the classification of clusters as "unused" based on less than complete surveys of all component nests may have added noise to our data due to potential misclassifications

Availability and Quality of Ancillary Data

We easily gathered basic well-location data from the Wyoming Oil and Gas Conservation Commission and Utah Division of Oil, Gas, and Mining web sites. We often found the records wanting, however, in terms of missing or incomplete data on development initiation and completion dates, and insufficient information concerning the timing and extent of maintenance activities and "workovers." In many cases, through significant effort we were able to fill-in the missing data by tracking down the original, individual well records; however, one problem that could not be eliminated effectively concerned what we presume to be discrepancies in reported and actual key activity dates (e.g., reported drilling dates that corresponded to approved targets rather than actual dates). For example, in both the Wyoming and Utah well records, we encountered well-completion dates that preceded spudding dates (i.e., initiation of drilling) by days to months.

We found that available road-network data layers were substantially lacking, especially concerning accurate and current representation of well-pad roads. Through hand digitizing of visible roads on 1-m-resolution aerial photographs taken in 2006 (U.S. Department of Agriculture National Agriculture Imagery Program), we added 270 km and 1,470 km of well-head roads, and an overall total of 1,063 km and 2,910 km of roads, in the Price and Rawlins study areas, respectively (Smith et al. 2010).

Although a product did become available late in the game, initially no useful, high-resolution vegetation map was available for the Rawlins study area. High-quality habitat maps are an essential backdrop for any study concerned with evaluating the landscape ecology of wildlife populations. Moreover, although we were eventually able to obtain high-quality vegetation maps for both study areas, the variation in the classification schemes employed in each study area required us to reduce the vegetation datasets to simpler, more compatible classifications. This was true even within the Rawlins study area, despite the fact that the same GIS laboratory produced both maps for this area. Unfortunately, this caused us to lose potentially valuable information about, for example, percentage sagebrush (*Artemisia* spp.) cover represented in the more detailed of the two Rawlins layers. Regardless, we found vegetation parameters were important in most models of nest use and activity (Smith et al. 2010).

Data available through the National Climatic Data Center (NOAA 2007) provided a means of representing coarse-scale, annual variation in regional climate and drought severity, which worked well as a covariate in our models to help account for interannual variation in overall ecosystem condition (Smith et al. 2010). However, the absence of finer-scale information (i.e., from multiple weather stations located in the study area) sufficient to portray, for example, spatial variation in precipitation levels within each study area, effectively precluded more insightful modeling of the interactive influences of habitat condition and development levels on nesting activity.

Nest-Cluster versus Nest-Centric Monitoring

Because most raptor species routinely use and maintain a series of alternative nest sites within their breeding territories, with use of individual nest sites varying from year to year in a variety of species-specific and individualized patterns, it is essential that monitoring of nesting activity be based on a territory or "nest-cluster" approach rather than a "nest-centric" approach. This is critical to allow for accurate representation of multi-year history and necessary distinction of truly inactive nests/territories from nests that are inactive only because that year the actual breeding attempt occurred at another nest in the cluster. In other words, the relationships among nests associated with a given nest cluster are not independent and highly misleading results may be obtained if they are treated as such. The problem is that accurate designation of distinct nest clusters requires several years of consistent monitoring to identify clearly the range of associated nests and cluster boundaries. In other words, properly setting the stage for evaluating the effects of specific disturbances or land-use changes on nesting dynamics requires a multi-year period of robust baseline monitoring to both clearly delineate the distribution of distinct nest clusters and provide indexes to pre-disturbance nest success and productivity patterns. Moreover, throughout any monitoring effort, it is essential that the focus always be on documenting whatever nesting activity is occurring in an area, not just on revisiting known nests, because new nests may be added to a territory and disused older nests may be refurbished and used again at any time. An apparent lack of attention to this facet of monitoring was abundantly apparent in the data from both the Price and Rawlins study areas, with nests that now clearly comprise single nest clusters often monitored inconsistently across years and, as a result, it was sometimes impossible to confidently determine from the records whether the cluster was in fact active or inactive in some years.

Baseline Monitoring

Perhaps the most serious limitation of both relevant datasets for evaluating the potential effects of OG development was a lack of robust, pre-development, baseline monitoring data. Such information is essential for accurately portraying the initial conditions that existed before widespread OG development began to affect the relevant ecosystems. Without such information,

it is essentially impossible to determine accurately the landscape-level impact of development on the community of nesting raptors and related ecosystem elements (i.e., potential changes in the number, species-specific composition, and reproductive output of nesting raptors). Moreover, even once intensive surveys were begun in the two study areas with the goal of gathering data that might help evaluate the potential impacts of development, inadequate attention was directed toward ensuring consistent, representative sampling of areas not yet affected by development. Again, this largely precluded effective evaluation of the comparative activity levels, success, and productivity of nest clusters exposed to development and not exposed to development, because the latter generally were monitored less consistently.

For example, our analyses occasionally suggested an apparent positive correlation between development proximity/density and cluster use or activity (Smith et al. 2010). Due to the absence of representative, pre-development, baseline data, there is no way to know whether this apparent positive association may be due to a correlation between development and higher quality nesting habitats, or if in fact the nesting raptors actually benefited from some aspect of development effects on the landscape. Moreover, if the former is the case, due to the lack of both pre-development baseline monitoring and effective, concurrent baseline monitoring in similar areas outside the development realm, we have no way to accurately discern whether nesting activity or success has changed due to development.

Another element of baseline monitoring that was wholly lacking for both study areas and comprises an essential element for effective evaluation of relationships between nesting raptors and their environment, whether affected by development pressures or not, is prey monitoring. Because prey ecology is a primary determinant of raptor nesting ecology (e.g., see Smith and Murphy [1979] and Steenhof et al. [1997]), without representative prey monitoring to facilitate understanding of how variation in prey abundance and accessibility interacts with development disturbance in affecting nesting raptors, it is very difficult to develop a confident assessment of development impacts.

Survey Extent and Timing

To derive an unbiased estimate of raptor nesting parameters within a study area or population requires monitoring that effectively encompasses a representative suite of nests, in terms of both spatial and temporal aspects, and reflects application of a consistent approach for all monitored nests. A critical facet of representative monitoring that is often overlooked or at least poorly achieved for various reasons concerns effective coverage to document initial territory occupation and early nesting failures. The available Price dataset was fundamentally flawed for this reason, because a single mid-season survey simply is not adequate to provide representative sampling of early season failures. On the one hand, the stated motivation for limiting the helicopter surveys to a later period to avoid unnecessary early season disturbance of nesting birds (C. Colt pers. comm.) may have been appropriate. On the other hand, not pursuing other less-intrusive, ground-based surveys to accomplish needed early season monitoring substantially limited the value of the data collected. Generally, beginning surveys in early to mid-March effectively encompasses the early season activities of most raptor species in the region of interest. The only diurnal species for which this may not be true are Bald Eagles (*Haliaeetus leucocephalus*) and Golden Eagles (*Aquila chrysaetos*), which in some years and areas of the interior west may begin nesting as early as January (e.g., Buehler 2000, Kochert et al. 2002, Keller 2005). One logistical problem that researchers may confront in accomplishing effective early season monitoring of these species is inaccessible roadways (due to snow cover, etc.), which ironically advocates for helicopter surveys (from a safe, non-intrusive vantage point), if that resource is available.

Although not as much of an issue relative to achieving representative sampling, ensuring adequate late-season coverage also is critical if robust nesting-success and productivity indexes are desired. The standard for deriving reliable estimates of nesting success and productivity for raptors requires confirmation of status once chicks have reached at least 80% of fledging age (Steenhof and Newton 2007). To accomplish this consistently, especially when species-specific timing within a given study area may vary by as much as several weeks, generally requires at least three visits per season to each nest. The first early season visit would be designed to document nest initiation or early incubation, and the second midseason visit would be designed ideally to confirm hatching and derive an initial age estimate for the chicks. These first two visits would then provide an essential basis for predicting when the chicks should reach 80% of fledging age, and therefore identify the window of opportunity for conducting the final visit to confirm nest success and productivity. Again, the single midseason visit that was the standard for the Price surveys substantially limited the value of these data because it effectively precluded evaluating relationships between

development patterns and nest success and productivity. Similarly, in the Rawlins area insufficient coverage and attention to the timing of follow-up visits often precluded reliable estimates of final nest success and productivity, especially for species other than the Ferruginous Hawk (historically the species of primary interest in this region).

Another facet of survey coverage that limited our investigations was inconsistent interannual survey histories for most nests and nest clusters. A well-designed, representative, randomized annual sampling regime could in theory support a wide variety of analyses designed to investigate the effects of land-use changes such as OG development, while reducing the effort required of field personnel. For example, such monitoring would support evaluating how study-area-wide nesting activity levels, nesting success, and productivity varied from year to year in relation to changing development levels or other aspects of changing habitat quality. Assuming the extent of surveys and development activity was sufficient to yield appropriate sample distributions, such a survey program may also support evaluation of facets such as how nesting activity varies with habitat type, in relation to time since proximate development occurred, or in relation to development proximity or density. Nevertheless, consistent, multi-year, pre- and post-development monitoring of representative suites of nest clusters may yield additional advantages. For example, such would allow for detection of relatively subtle responses to development such as changes in the locations of "preferred" nest sites or long-term changes in the frequency of nesting within clusters. In many cases, such an approach may also prove valuable because the cluster sample sizes needed to support robust statistical analyses under a repeated-measures, pre- and post-development tracking scenario would generally be less than for a randomized, multi-year sampling scenario.

Problems HWI Identified Concerning Raptor-Related Management of OG Development Activities

Based on our collective experiences working in the Rawlins Field Office for several years (M. Neal), brief exposure to on-going raptor surveys in the Price study area, and our recent work developing plans for and assessing the efficacy of implementing Phase II of the Raptor Radii Project across study areas in Utah, Wyoming, and Colorado, below we identify some of the key issues pertaining to management of OG development activities and overall raptor management in the study area:

- Inconsistent application of raptor stipulations across and within management areas.

- Field personnel are not always adequately trained in the collection of standardized field data and the subtleties of terminology, nest-observation and nest-relocation protocols, and record keeping necessary for rigorous monitoring of raptor nesting activity.

- Field-Office biologists frequently do not have adequate time or resources available to them to accomplish the intensive monitoring of raptors and associated landscape conditions required for robust analyses of energy-development effects on nesting raptors.

- Adequate BLM and industry resources are necessary to assure a clear understanding by both about the required stipulations and to ensure there are no disconnects among agency personnel, industry planners, and the personnel actually responsible for conducting operations on the ground. Individuals at the site must be aware of specific stipulations or conditions, raptor nest locations, and other protected resources associated with a development site.

- Many current RMPs and management plans require no spatial disturbance buffers outside of the breeding season or outside the development stage. As a result, nests sometimes are destroyed, but more frequently are rendered unusable due to the proximity of development allowed to occur between breeding seasons, regardless of nest-use history. Additionally, current stipulations rarely account for continued disturbance activities that occur during the production phase of an OG project.

- On-site visits to assess the merits of industry exception, waiver, or modification requests often occur too early in the nesting season to ensure accurate assessments of nesting activity.

- Re-use intervals for specific nests and nest clusters often extend to several years or more; however, some agency management scenarios allow for nest spatial-buffer encroachment following as few as three years of apparent inactivity.

- Whether intentional or inadvertent, misclassification of nest status (e.g., used or unused for reproduction in a given year) has serious consequences for raptor conservation efforts and for evaluating the efficacy of management actions. Field biologists should establish unambiguous criteria for assessing nest status and develop categories for data that clearly indicate the manner by which surveyors assign a use category to a nest.

Recommendations for Improved Monitoring

Presented below are HWI's recommendations for improved monitoring of nesting raptors, which draw on the conclusions presented in our previous overview of the existing data and the survey limitations we experienced during the course of this study. HWI recognizes that BLM Field Offices and personnel frequently are faced with limited resources with which to conduct wildlife and other types of surveys. In this light, we present the following recommendations for an ideal, comprehensive monitoring strategy, and highlight the most important and minimum-necessary components to help land managers establish monitoring priorities.

To set the stage effectively for rigorously evaluating the impacts on nesting raptors of a new, planned disturbance, such as OG development, requires solid baseline inventory and monitoring data. The following comprise HWI's recommendations for necessary and desired characteristics of baseline monitoring and associated survey protocols needed to facilitate robust evaluations of the effects of land-use practices on nesting raptors in landscapes typical of those managed by the BLM in the interior western United States. Most of the described characteristics also would apply equally well to monitoring that would need to occur during and after application of relevant disturbance regimes or development activities.

Pre-development monitoring period: 3–5 years, optimally, or as many years as possible prior to the onset of energy development activities.

Required to:

- Enable effective, initial delineation of nest clusters.

- Accommodate typically intermittent nesting of species such as Golden Eagles.

- Allow reasonable time for capturing territory turnover and reoccupancy of abandoned territories by other species.

- Obtain reasonable baseline data on species-specific population densities, habitat associations, and nest success and productivity rates for the study area prior to development.

Spatial domain: extending 5–10 km outside of proposed development area with comparable representation of habitats.

Required to:

- Enable adequate identification of nest clusters that may overlap the development area.

- Provide reference or "control" monitoring data for comparing against data from the development area. Satisfying this need may not require a comprehensive, radial extension of the survey area, but may require careful attention to selecting areas and an overall geographic extent beyond the development area that provides comparable coverage of habitats and sufficient nest-cluster sample sizes within those habitats for all focal species to support robust control–treatment statistical analyses.

Data requirements:

1) Comprehensive nest inventory for a representative suite of species (i.e., reflecting a reasonable range of ecologies and expected sensitivities to disturbance).

    - The choice of which species to focus on may vary depending on:

        a) The species known to occur in the area, their conservation status, and prior knowledge of their relative abundance in the area.

        b) The nature of the planned development/disturbance (i.e., what habitats will be affected, nocturnal versus diurnal activities, hypothesized impacts, spacing of disturbance, etc.).

        c) Logistical considerations and practical constraints with regard to the efficacy of gathering robust monitoring data for certain species.

- The inventory database should include the following information, initially recorded on standardized field data forms (which are carefully and meticulously archived) and then transferred to an appropriate, electronic, relational database system compatible with a GIS:

a) A unique nest name/number that does not include a species designation but does help place the nest geographically at a relatively fine-scale; e.g., includes a Township-Range-Section designation or a code indicating the 7.5' topographic map within which the nest lies.

b) Precise (±3–4 m or better) GPS location coordinates for all nest sites recorded in a consistent coordinate system (preferably UTM coordinates using a consistent datum; i.e., NAD27 or NAD83), with meticulous metadata recorded concerning the resolution of the GPS device, coordinate system, and datum used. For nests located on high cliffs or in locations that otherwise preclude direct access to the nest or positions directly above or below the nest for acquisition of accurate nest coordinates, coordinates should be recorded from the closest accessible point near the nest and combined with a bearing reading and distance estimate derived from a laser rangefinder. In such cases, hand plotting of the estimated nest location on a 7.5' topographic map may also help refine the location data upon plotting within a GIS. Although we recognize that not all monitoring programs may be able to achieve the same levels of accuracy and that some situations preclude the accurate recording of locations, we advocate that surveyors record locations with the highest feasible accuracy and keep clear records concerning said accuracy levels.

c) Township-Range-Section-Quarter Section location information whenever known to serve as back-up location data in case of error in recording GPS coordinates.

d) GPS coordinates for "ideal" viewing of nests from a distance (to avoid unnecessary disturbance, early season monitoring requires viewing from at least 400–800 m away, depending on the species).

e) Field drawn map and/or verbal description of the nest location relative to proximate roads, other relevant features (e.g., topographic or vegetation features), and view coordinates.

f) Substrate type and height above ground. Descriptions of nest substrate should be as detailed as possible (e.g., the species of tree, or at least evergreen or deciduous, rather than simply "tree") to facilitate nest re-location and insights on the relative value of different substrates in the project area and their vulnerability to OG development.

g) Nest type (e.g., stick nest or scrape), estimated size (height, width, depth), location on substrate (top of tree, lateral branch, cliff ledge or pothole, etc.), height above ground, direction of exposure to and degree/nature of protection from the elements, accessibility to humans and ground-based predators, and current condition. A basic estimation of nest size (we are not advocating for the actual physical measurement of individual nests) can be helpful in distinguishing between proximate nests and in determining the likely species associations of inactive nests. Although assessment of nest accessibility is subjective, this assessment is critical to assessing the relative value and vulnerability of various nest substrates to development, as well as to potential nest predators. Such information may also aid in planning for equipment needed to conduct detailed nest checks for productivity assessments or to plan additional research that requires handling chicks (e.g., for health monitoring or banding).

h) Notes on known or hypothesized relationships to other proximal nests; i.e., is the nest believed to be part of a larger nest cluster.

i) Standardized assessment of the primary habitat types and conditions surrounding the nest at 1-km radius.

j) A series of high-resolution digital photos taken at various distances from the nest (including data on the location from which each photo was taken and the estimated distance and bearing to the nest) to facilitate future relocation and provide a photographic record of the structural and location characteristics of each nest.

2) Annual monitoring data for all known and newly discovered nests for all focal species.

- During the pre-development inventory and monitoring period (ideally 3–5 years), monitoring data should be spatially comprehensive to facilitate accurate delineation of nest clusters, habitat relationships, climate effects, and associated population dynamics. Once a solid, comprehensive inventory and initial monitoring database has been compiled, it then should be possible to develop a spatially less-intensive but representative sampling regime for gathering future monitoring data that will allow for effective evaluation of the effects of development activities.

- An ideal monitoring regime should include a minimum of three visits to all nests/nest clusters, with the timing depending on the species involved. Simply documenting nest activity does not provide land managers with an adequate tool to assess the potential negative impacts of disturbances such as OG development; i.e., active nests that subsequently fail are indistinguishable from successful nests, and successful nests in different habitats/development scenarios may experience different levels of productivity.

a. For most species (e.g., Bald and Golden Eagles, Red-tailed and Ferruginous Hawks, Prairie Falcons [*Falco mexicanus*], and Peregrine Falcons [*F. peregrinus*]) first visits should occur from March through early April to document initial territory occupancy, courtship and nest-building/tending activities, and preferably actual nest-

initiation (i.e., egg laying and initial incubation). Although earlier visits for early-nesting species such as the Golden Eagle may be valuable for the detection of early nest failures, such visits are often logistically infeasible. For other late-nesting species, such as Swainson's Hawks (*Buteo swainsoni*) and Burrowing Owls (*Athene cunicularia*), nest initiation typically does not occur until late April through May, so the timing of first visits would need to be adjusted accordingly. To avoid unnecessary disturbance during the most sensitive period in the nesting cycle, observers should attempt to achieve most early nest monitoring activities at distances of at least 800 m (0.5 mile) from nests of most raptor species. We suggest this distance as a general rule of thumb and recognize that closer observation of some species, such as the American Kestrel (*Falco sparverius*), Barn Owl (*Tyto alba*), and Prairie Falcon, may be acceptable, while endangered or threatened species should be given a wider berth (Romin and Muck 2002). We also suggest that nest-viewing distances may be adjusted based on the specific conditions at a particular nest (e.g., topography, vegetation screening, etc.). Regardless, this type of relatively long-distance monitoring is dependent on the use of high-quality spotting scopes and often extended observation periods to acquire accurate information. Ensuring adequate early season monitoring is the most critical component of any survey regime, because deriving an accurate index of annual nesting activity requires knowledge of early failures, which cannot be gleaned from only mid- or late-season monitoring. These visits should focus on both revisiting all known nesting areas and observing for signs of activity in other areas of suitable habitat that may not have been used or known as nesting areas previously.

b. Second, mid-season visits are designed ideally to confirm hatching success or failure and to obtain initial age estimates for chicks and initial brood sizes. These visits also provide the first opportunities to safely intrude more closely into nesting habitats to identify other nesting that may have been missed during distant, early-season monitoring. These visits typically should occur from mid-April through early June, depending on the species and indications of cycle timing derived from early season visits. We consider these first two visits the minimum necessary to confirm annual numbers of breeding events in a study area.

c. Third visits are designed to confirm nesting success and productivity. They should be timed based on knowledge of egg-laying or hatching dates to allow for confirmation of nestlings reaching 80% of the average fledging age for the species. Waiting until after chicks are likely to have fledged may still yield confirmation of nesting success if one or more fledglings are found in the area, they can be accurately distinguished from adults, and there is no chance of confusing fledglings from different nests, but often precludes accurate confirmation of productivity (i.e., the actual number of chicks fledged). These third visits may be considered discretionary if the monitoring objective is limited to documenting annual breeding levels; however, doing so will substantially limit the value of inferences drawn concerning effects of development. We suggest that the minimum strategy should entail confirming nesting success.

• All monitoring data must conform to standardized and meticulously documented terminology standards and recording protocols (see Steenhof and Newton [2007] for further guidance), and be collected by adequately trained personnel to ensure long-term consistency and conformity to the adopted standards. This may require annual training of new or inexperienced employees. Along with being familiar with terminology standards presented in Steenhof and Newton (2007), we suggest that field personnel also have a basic understanding of species-specific raptor behaviors and nesting ecology, which can easily be gleaned from reviewing relevant Birds of North America accounts (see http://bna.birds.cornell.edu/BNA). It is particularly

important to adopt and ensure conformity to rigorous standards designed to distinguish "occupied" and "unoccupied" nest clusters or territories, and to confirm actual breeding events (i.e., eggs laid):

a. Whether or not an actual breeding event occurs, identification of "occupied" nest clusters ideally should be based on repeated observations of one or more breeding-age adults in the immediate vicinity of the nest cluster, preferably combined with evidence of territorial behavior, courtship/pair-bonding activities, and/or nest tending. Digital photo records of nests from the previous year may assist in identifying recently "improved" or "tended" nests through comparison of nest sizes, the nature of materials present, and whitewash signs. Otherwise, absent actual observations of an adult at or working on a nest, one must be very careful in classifying nests as tended or occupied without multiple lines of evidence supporting such a classification. For example, perceived additions of new nest material or the presence of apparently fresh whitewash are not sufficient evidence alone, as both can be very difficult to discern depending on lighting, viewing angles, and the relative exposure of the nest to the elements. In addition, use of certain nests by more than one species in different years is common, particularly where buteo and raven nests are concerned, so one must also be careful not to assign activity to a former species in the absence of confirming use by that species in the current year. Positive evidence of nest tending also does not confirm an actual breeding event.

b. Confirmation of an actual breeding event must be based on evidence that egg laying occurred. Such evidence may include direct confirmation of eggs or chicks in the nest (or perhaps freshly hatched or broken eggs or dead chicks under the nest), witnessing an obviously incubating adult, prey deliveries to the nest and/or obvious chick-feeding behavior, and as a last resort obvious late-season signs that the nest was occupied for a long period by nestlings (e.g., heavy, fresh whitewash deposits, extensive prey remains, and/or obvious downy chick feathers in or under the nest).

3) Annual, representative prey-monitoring data.

- Prey abundance and accessibility often are the primary drivers of raptor nesting activity and especially success and productivity (Smith and Murphy 1979, Steenhof et al. 1997, Smith et al. 2010). Therefore, an absence of knowledge concerning spatial and temporal patterns and trends in prey availability may seriously compromise efforts to evaluate accurately the impacts of other factors such as OG development on a population. Achieving adequate and truly representative prey monitoring often is a very challenging proposition, however, and so rarely has been achieved, especially at larger landscape scales. It is not our goal here to advocate one particular survey method over another, but rather point out that various techniques exist for these species and that, whenever feasible, prey monitoring should be considered an integral part of any raptor nest-monitoring program.

- The choice of what prey species to monitor may depend on the focal raptor species of interest; however, we suggest that targeting a few key species or species groups generally should provide a well-rounded assessment of relevant prey-composition and trends that will be useful for at least typical diurnal raptor communities in the interior West. These include:

  a. Rabbits and hares. Throughout much of the interior West, black-tailed jackrabbits (*Lepus californicus*), white-tailed jackrabbits (*Lepus townsendii*), and various cottontail species (*Sylvilagus* spp.) are of great importance to Golden Eagles (Kochert et al. 2002). Snowshoe Hares (*Lepus arcticus*) are an important prey species for raptors at higher latitudes and elevations. Various techniques are available for surveying rabbits and hares, including nighttime spotlighting on road transects (e.g., Smith and Nydeggar 1985), walking transects (e.g., Gross et

al. 1974), pellet counts (e.g., Prugh and Krebs 2004), and more intensive mark-recapture techniques.

  b. Squirrels. Ground squirrels (*Spermophilus spp.*) and prairie dogs (*Cynomys spp.*) in open habitats and tree squirrels in forested habitats constitute important prey items for many medium-sized raptors such as buteos, the larger accipiters, and Prairie Falcons, as well as Golden Eagles. Visual animal counts may be more effective than burrow counts for both prairie dogs and ground squirrels (see Van Horne et al. [1997] and Severson and Plumb [1998]). Walking transects for visual and/or aural detections may be useful for monitoring tree squirrels (e.g., Burnham et al. 1980).

  c. Small rodents. Various mice, voles, and rats are key constituents in the diets of many small to medium-sized raptors. Various types of live or lethal trapping arrays are effective tools for monitoring the species diversity and abundance patterns of this group of species (e.g., Pearson and Ruggiero 2003).

  d. Birds. A variety of birds are important prey species for many raptors, ranging from primarily small songbirds for species such as the Sharp-shinned Hawk (*Accipiter striatus*) and American Kestrel, to larger grouse and pheasants for eagles, goshawks, and some larger buteos. Visual and aural point counts are an effective method for monitoring species occurrence and the relative abundance of communities of especially small to medium sized birds (e.g., Reynolds et al. 1980), whereas walking transects are often the most productive method for surveying species such as grouse and pheasants.

- Once a representative array of species or species groups is selected for prey monitoring, decisions must be made about the nature of data desired. To be useful, prey monitoring should minimally provide robust, study-area-wide, annual indexes of relative abundance for each focal species or species group to help account for annual variation in raptor nesting activity, success, and productivity related to this important factor. Ideally, sampling also would provide for discrimination of relative prey diversity and abundance across different habitat types or otherwise distinct segments of the study-area landscape that are relevant to nesting raptors. During or after development has occurred, an appropriate sampling regime may be to target areas around subsets of "control" and "treatment" nest clusters for each focal raptor species to provide comparative data for modeling landscape characteristic around each.

4) Annual, representative climatic and landscape-condition data.

- Annual climatic summary data for general landscape regions across the U.S. are generally readily available through the National Climatic Data Center, and can serve well in providing monthly to annual indexes of general climatic conditions (e.g., drought severity levels and precipitation totals) in the region of interest.

- Finer-scale information sufficient to discriminate variation in, for example, moisture and drought severity levels across habitat types would further assist in accounting for (in a modeling sense) the effects of within-study area variation in habitat condition that is unrelated to the disturbance factor of interest. Acquiring such data would require, however, placement of a representative array of automated weather stations throughout the study-area landscape, which may be cost prohibitive.

- Accurate, annual mapping of fire histories can be another important tool for qualifying landscape condition.

- Standardized, annual assessments of range condition may be another effective means for helping to quantify annual and potentially within-study-area spatial variability in landscape condition. Effective, spatially explicit tracking of annual livestock stocking levels also may be of great interest, as landscape alterations from livestock grazing can significantly alter the distribution and abundance of key raptor prey species.

- If other forms of human disturbance are prevalent in the study area (e.g., recreational activities, wind farms, quarries, etc.), annual, spatially explicit monitoring and quantification of such activities also may be important to provide a truly robust basis for evaluating the effects of a new disturbance such as OG development.

5) Other desired GIS data layers describing the study-area landscape:

- High-quality 10–30-m resolution vegetation/landcover data layer(s) derived from classified satellite imagery. At least one representative and reasonably contemporary map is essential, but multiple versions prepared to represent change at 3–5-year intervals are ideal. When the BLM funds the preparation of GIS data layers such as these, we suggest that careful attention be paid to existing layers to avoid the loss of information that necessarily occurs when attempting to combine data with different levels of detail and varying classification schemes. We recognize that the continual improvement in the resolution of aerial and remote sensing data should naturally lead to more detailed and refined data layers; however, we suggest that if some attention is paid to previously used classification schemes, it could facilitate the more direct linking of various datasets (e.g., greater refinement in newer datasets might simply be represented by sub-classifications of previously used schemes).

- Minimum 30-m resolution Digital Elevation Model to represent landscape topography.

- Current, comprehensive road-network data layer, with all roads classified in terms of type (e.g., primary paved, secondary gravel, dirt two-track, oil and gas road, etc.), and preferably including dates of first appearance or construction, and some indication of relative traffic levels.

- Current, comprehensive data layer representing the distribution of power and telephone lines, with lines classified by type (e.g., high-voltage transmission, distribution, etc.).

- Current, comprehensive OG well-location data layer, with all wells classified by type (oil, conventional natural gas, coalbed methane, etc.), and including accurate and precise construction, spudding, major workover, and capping dates, as relevant.

Survey Methods

In our experience, ground-based surveys generally are the most cost-effective, efficient, and least disturbing means of obtaining accurate monitoring data for multiple species. This is particularly true if any species other than eagles or Ferruginous Hawks are targeted, because most other species are simply too cryptic for aerial surveys to be productive. That said, if managed appropriately, aerial surveys, particularly helicopter surveys, can be a very efficient and productive, though very costly, tool for surveying species such as eagles and in many cases Ferruginous Hawks, whose large nests are generally located in situations where they can be seen easily from the air. Moreover, aerial surveys may be a particularly useful tool to achieve early-season monitoring in areas where snow cover or otherwise poor road conditions preclude easy access early in the year. Aerial surveys may also be particularly useful for gaining visual confirmation of the contents of highly elevated nests. With this said, research has documented the potential for nest disturbance associated with close passage of aircraft, although some species may habituate to this type of disturbance relatively quickly (Andersen et al. 1989). Perhaps more importantly, the high cost of helicopter surveys, and specifically the cost of time spent in the air, may limit the rigor and thoroughness of aerial survey programs."

The observational period required to determine nest status depends on the species and nest situation. During early season monitoring when nests cannot be approached closely or whenever the nest location precludes direct observation of nest contents or easy detection of an incubating adult on the nest from an appropriate distant vantage point, a minimum 1-hour observation period will usually be required to confirm the status of the nest through observation of nest switching by incubating adults, an adult adjusting its position on the nest, or, during brood-rearing, the chicks standing up to stretch or adjust their positions or the adults bringing prey. However, the necessary observation period may need to extend to two hours for species such as Peregrine Falcons when they are nesting in hidden cliff cavities. Additionally, once both adults can be away from the nest to forage for their chicks, observation periods of several

hours may be required to confirm the status of Golden Eagles nests.

Besides a high-quality spotting scope and mounting system, binoculars, a digital camera, a reliable handheld GPS unit, a laser range finder, and a compass, another very important survey tool relevant to gathering accurate nest-monitoring data is a telescoping mirror pole (4–5 m extension range) that can be used to inspect the contents of many nests from above or below.

Continued Monitoring

After initial baseline data have been collected, nests should be assigned to clusters based on proximity and history of use. Ideally, all known clusters should be monitored (within and outside the development project boundary) as development proceeds. If comprehensive annual monitoring is not achievable, we would instead advocate use of representative random sampling of known nesting areas on an annual basis, with the sampling regime designed to achieve the following:

- Annual monitoring of at least 15–20 nest clusters representing each species, primary habitat types, and both "control" and "treatment" regions. These sample sizes reflect the minimum number necessary to detect changes in nest productivity of 50% or more between groups (i.e., control and treatment nests), as suggested by statistical power analysis and fledgling-production effects sizes estimated from five years of intensive nest monitoring data collected for the same species by HWI in the northern Great Basin of Utah and Nevada (Smith and Hutchins 2006, 2007). Note that this approach still requires an initial gathering of relatively complete, area-wide baseline information to facilitate the selection of cluster samples.

- Both re-checking of known nesting areas and nest clusters, and searches for potential new nests in suitable areas. A quadrat-based sampling strategy should be able to provide insight into general habitat conditions, nesting densities, and reproductive output based on a subsample of the full landscape.

- Representative subsets of species-specific nest clusters that are monitored every year to obtain information about consistency of cluster use and nest-switching rates.

- Either sampling that ensures all areas are re-inventoried at least every five years, or alternatively that a comprehensive re-inventory occurs every five years, to maintain accurate and current knowledge of all nest locations across the landscape of interest.

- Representative annual monitoring as long as development activity continues to expand across the landscape of interest, and continuation for at least another 3–5 years following cessation of new development activity to provide for an assessment of stabilization tendencies.

Otherwise, standardized monitoring of prey populations and other landscape-condition indices should continue on an annual basis along side any raptor monitoring that occurs. Augmentation of effort or sampling locations to better correspond to specific "treatment" locations may be desired at this stage, if resources allow and it is relevant to achieving research objectives associated with evaluating the effects of development or other human activities. Additionally, longer-term post-development monitoring also may be desirable, if the evaluation of the potential efficacy of post-development reclamation activities also is a goal of the monitoring program.

Lastly, HWI recommends that protecting historic nest sites, especially those with a lengthy history of use, should be considered a priority regardless of the current condition of the actual nest or the length of time the nest has been inactive. Even when historic nests become highly degraded or collapse entirely, that site may still be preferentially chosen by new breeders for re-occupation and rebuilding because it is a particularly attractive location. While we recognize that it may be impractical to protect all nest sites indefinitely, we do suggest that protections be extended to account for potential fluctuations in nest activity as related to prey abundance, climatic fluctuations, etc. (e.g., Romin and Muck [2002] advocate for protection of inactive nests for at least seven years).

Recommendations on the Recording and Storage of Data

During the course of our own (HWI) nest survey efforts, we created and refined field datasheets which can be used to facilitate the recording of nest and nest-site characteristics previously outlined in the Improved Monitoring section. We provide example datasheets in Appendix A, which may be used directly by field personnel or as a template to guide the production of similar datasheets for specific monitoring programs. We also developed a Microsoft Access relational database system for storing and querying nest location and monitoring data; a template of this database system is readily available to any interested parties at http://www.hawkwatch.org/conservation-science/tools-and-resources. We strongly advocate that any nest-monitoring plan also budget time and personnel for regular electronic entry of data to facilitate ease of data retrieval and use in conjunction with other data layers and mapping software. Collected data should be archived in both hardcopy and electronic form, preferably in distinct physical locations, to prevent the potential complete loss of data. We also recommend that detailed metadata accompany the database and any database or mapping products derived from the collected data. Detailed metadata should serve to reduce the likelihood of the unintentional misinterpretation or misuse of collected data and associated products. Perhaps more importantly, it should also facilitate the maintenance of consistent data-collection standards and the continued, effective implementation of established monitoring programs, even in the face of potential turnover of field and program-oversight personnel.

Andersen, D. E., O. J. Rongstad, and W. R. Mytton. 1989. Response of nesting Red-tailed Hawks to helicopter overflights. Condor 91:296–299.

Buehler, D. A. 2000. Bald Eagle (*Haliaeetus leucocephalus*). No. 506 *in* A. Poole and F. Gill (Editors), The birds of North America. The Birds of North America, Inc., Philadelphia, PA U.S.A.

Burnham, K. P., D. R. Anderson, and J. L. Laake. 1980. Estimation of density from line transect sampling of biological populations. Wildlife Monographs 72:1–202.

Gross, J. E., L. C. Stoddart, and F. H. Wagner. 1974. Demographic analysis of a northern Utah jackrabbit population. Wildlife Monographs 40:1–68.

Keller, K. 2005. Golden Eagle nesting survey report for the central Utah study area: February - July 2004. Contract report submitted to the Utah Division of Wildlife Resources, Salt Lake City, UT U.S.A.

Kochert, M. N., K. Steenhof, C. L. McIntyre, and E. H. Craig. 2002. Golden Eagle (*Aquila chrysaetos*). No. 506 *in* A. Poole and F. Gill (Editors), The birds of North America. The Birds of North America, Inc., Philadelphia, PA U.S.A.

National Oceanic and Atmospheric Administration (NOAA). 2007. National climatic data center. On-line at http://www7.ncdc.noaa.gov/CDO/ CDODivisionalSelect.jsp#. Last accessed May 2007.

Pearson, D. E., and L. F. Ruggiero. 2003. Transect versus grid trapping arrangements for sampling small-mammal communities. Wildlife Society Bulletin 31:454–459.

Prugh, L. R., and C. J. Krebs. 2004. Snowshoe hare pellet-decay rates and aging in different habitats. Wildlife Society Bulletin 32:386–393.

Reynolds, R. T., J. M. Scott, and R. A. Nussbaum. 1980. A variable circular-plot method for estimating bird numbers. Condor 82:309–313.

Romin, L. A., and J. A. Muck. 2002. Utah Field Office guidelines for raptor protection from human and land use disturbances. U.S. Fish and Wildlife Service, Utah Field Office, Salt Lake City, UT U.S.A. 42 pp.

Severson, K. E., and G. E. Plumb. 1998. Comparison of methods to estimate population densities of black-tailed prairie dogs. Wildlife Society Bulletin 26:859–866.

Smith, J. P., and A. Hutchins. 2006. Northeast Nevada raptor nest survey 2005. HawkWatch International, Inc., Salt Lake City, UT U.S.A. 34 pp.

Smith, J. P., and A. Hutchins. 2007. Northwest Utah raptor nest survey 2006. HawkWatch International, Inc., Salt Lake City, UT U.S.A. 39 pp.

Smith, D. G., and J. R. Murphy. 1979. Breeding responses of raptors to jackrabbit density in the eastern Great Basin Desert of Utah. Raptor Research 13:1–14.

Smith, G. W., and N. C. Nydeggar. 1985. A spotlight, line-transect method for surveying jackrabbits. Journal of Wildlife Management 49:699–702.

Smith, J. P., S. J. Slater, and M. C. Neal. 2010. An assessment of the effects of oil and gas field activities on nesting raptors in the Rawlins, Wyoming, and Price, Utah, Field Offices of the Bureau of Land Management. Technical Note No. 433. USDI Bureau of Land Management, Utah State Office, Salt Lake City, UT, Wyoming State Office, Cheyenne, WY, and Colorado State Office, Lakewood, CO U.S.A.

Steenhof, K., M. N. Kochert, and T. L. MacDonald. 1997. Interactive effects of prey and weather on Golden Eagle reproduction. Journal of Animal Ecology 66:350–362.

Steenhof, K., and I. Newton. 2007. Assessing nesting success and productivity. Pages 181–192 *in* D. M. Bird and K. L. Bildstein (Editors), Raptor research and management techniques. Hancock House Publishers, Surrey, British Columbia, Canada, and Blaine, WA U.S.A.

Van Horne, B., R. L. Schooley, S. T. Knick, G. S. Olson, and K. P. Burnham. 1997. Use of burrow entrances to indicate densities of Townsend's ground squirrels. Journal of Wildlife Management 61:92–101.

Appendix A.
Example field datasheets
for raptor nest monitoring.

Raptor Nest Location Data Form

Nest No. _____

Species: _____   Status (active, inactive, unknown): _____

Territory Name (if known): _____

Observer(s): _____   Date Discovered: _____

7.5' Topo Quad Name: _____   Topo Code: _____

Township: _____ Range: _____ Section: _____ Quarter Section: _____ Elevation: _____ (m)

GPS model used: _____   UTM Nest Coords: _____ Zone _____ E _____ N

UTM View Coords: _____ E _____ N   Orientation / Distance to Nest: _____

Land ownership (indicate owner/manager name when known):

Private: _____   State: _____   Federal: _____

Specific directions to nest site: _____

_____

_____

_____

Map showing directions to nest site.

Digital Photos

Type	Camera	Photo#	Orientation
L1			
L2			
L3			
N			

Figure A1. Example "nest location" data form (front [previous page] and back [this page] sides) used to record detailed nest and nest-site characteristics of newly found raptor nest. Editable electronic versions of this data form are available at http://www.hawkwatch.org (find download link associated with listing of this manuscript in the publications section accessed from the Conservation Science menu).

General Description of Nest Site:

Substrate (e.g., cliff or outcrop [rock type], tree/shrub [species, live/dead], ground, artificial structure [type]):

_____

Estimated height of substrate: _____(m)   Estimated height of nest above ground: _____(m)

Nest type and location on substrate (e.g., stick nest in upper/lower canopy stick nest on/in ledge, pothole, or crevice; scrape on/in ledge, pothole, or crevice; stick nest on artificial platform mounted in tree; tree cavity; burrow; etc.):

_____

Protection from weather (YES/NO; describe nature of protection, e.g., tree canopy, cliff backdrop, pothole/crevice, burrow, etc.):

_____

Approximate compass direction of exposure to elements (wind, sun, etc.): _____

Describe visibility and accessibility of nest (relative to obtaining accurate status/productivity data, possibility for banding or nestling exams, searching for prey remains, and accessibility for predators, etc.):

_____

_____

_____

Nest size—indicate whether estimated or measured: _____

Height (top to bottom)_____ Width (left to right)_____ Depth (back to front)_____ (meters)

Known or probable alternative nests within territory and associated nest #'s:

_____

_____

Standard description of habitat types and land uses within 1-km radius of nest using UDWR classification codes and estimates of percentages of each habitat type within area, and any additional notes about apparent habitat condition:

_____

_____

_____

Additional notes about human activity within 1-km radius of nest (e.g., heavy road traffic, density of homes, recreational activities, etc.):

_____

_____

_____

_____

_____

Miscellaneous Notes:

_____

_____

_____

_____

_____

Raptor Nest History Data Form

Nest #_____   Page ___ of ___

Date (mm/dd/yy): _____   Observer(s): _____

Observation Begin Time: _____   End Time: _____ (24-hr clock, Local Standard Time only)

Species: _____   Time to confirmation of active status: _____

Status (courtship, nest building, incubating, nestlings, fledglings, occupied inactive territory, inactive territory and nest, unknown,): _____

Dead Eggs: _____ # Live eggs: _____ # Dead young: _____ # Live young: _____ Nest poled? Y / N

Estimated Ages of Young (days): _____ # Banded: _____

Basis for age of young (describe plumage and/or behavior): _____

_____

Description of adult activity: _____

_____

****

Date (mm/dd/yy): _____   Observer(s): _____

Observation Begin Time: _____   End Time: _____ (24-hr clock, Local Standard Time only)

Species: _____   Time to confirmation of active status: _____

Status (courtship, nest building, incubating, nestlings, fledglings, occupied inactive territory, inactive territory and nest, unknown,): _____

Dead Eggs: _____ # Live eggs: _____ # Dead young: _____ # Live young: _____ Nest poled? Y / N

Estimated Ages of Young (days): _____ # Banded: _____

Basis for age of young (describe plumage and/or behavior): _____

Description of adult activity: _____

_____

****

Date (mm/dd/yy): _____   Observer(s): _____

Observation Begin Time: _____   End Time: _____ (24-hr clock, Local Standard Time only)

Species: _____   Time to confirmation of active status: _____

Status (courtship, nest building, incubating, nestlings, fledglings, occupied inactive territory, inactive territory and nest, unknown,): _____

Dead Eggs: _____ # Live eggs: _____ # Dead young: _____ # Live young: _____ Nest poled? Y / N

Estimated Ages of Young (days): _____ # Banded: _____

Basis for age of young (describe plumage and/or behavior): _____

Description of adult activity: _____

_____

****

Date (mm/dd/yy): _____   Observer(s): _____

Observation Begin Time: _____   End Time: _____ (24-hr clock, Local Standard Time only)

Species: _____   Time to confirmation of active status: _____

Status (courtship, nest building, incubating, nestlings, fledglings, occupied inactive territory, inactive territory and nest, unknown,): _____

Dead Eggs: _____ # Live eggs: _____ # Dead young: _____ # Live young: _____ Nest poled? Y / N

Estimated Ages of Young (days): _____ # Banded: _____

Basis for age of young (describe plumage and/or behavior): _____

Description of adult activity: _____

_____

Figure A2. Example "nest history" data form (front [previous page] and back [this page] sides) used to record data from multiple nest-check visits. Editable electronic versions of this data form are available at http://www.hawkwatch.org (find download link associated with listing of this manuscript in the publications section accessed from the Conservation Science menu).

Nest condition (poor, fair, good, excellent, gone, collapsed, burned, etc.):

Date				
Condition				

Comments_____

_____

_____

Human activities:

Date			Date	
Activity			Activity	
Vehicle Types			Vehicle Types	
# of People/Vehicle			# of People/Vehicle	

Comments with observation dates and times, please record any signs of non-observed human activity and any bird reactions:

_____

_____

_____

_____

Habitat Condition and Changes (Please record developing conditions and changes to habitat in nest area such as fire or clearing):

_____

_____

_____

Prey Observations (for each potential species observed):

At Nest:

Date	Species	Abundance or #	Remains	Comments

General observations of prey distribution and abundance around nest area, and notes about raptor foraging/feeding in area:

_____

_____

_____

_____

These five documents are an integrated series.

BLM Technical Note 432	Raptor Nesting Near Oil and Gas Development: An Overview of Key Findings and Implications for Management Based on Four Reports by Hawk Watch International
BLM Technical Note 433	An Assessment of the Effects of Oil and Gas Field Activities on Nesting Raptors in the Rawlins, Wyoming and Price, Utah Field Offices of the Bureau of Land Management
BLM Technical Note 434	Artificial Nest Structures as Mitigation for Natural-Gas Development Impacts to Ferruginous Hawks (Buteo regalis) in South-Central Wyoming
BLM Technical Note 435	Accipiter Use of Pinyon–Juniper Habitats for Nesting in Northwestern Colorado
BLM Technical Note 436	Recommendations for Improved Raptor Nest Monitoring in Association with Oil and Gas Development Activities